For the Love of Tom

A Caregivers
Survival Guide

Of Faith, Hope and Love

"Live with purpose. Inspiring others to make a difference."
Anita M. Yelton

Anita M. Yelton, M.Ed. *BWE, Certified Coach, Facilitator, Trainer, Speaker, and Caregiver

Jessica McMullin Prior Certified Coach, Trainer, Speaker, Certified Children and Family Advisor

Table of Contents

Dedication

In loving memory of my precious Tom, our two children, Ty Yelton and Tami McMullin who made it possible to keep Tom at home until his final breath, and our grandchildren who stayed with us those final days and hours. Praying this book will be an inspiration to caregivers everywhere.

To Jessi, who started as my editor and became a valuable resource and co-author of this book. Your ability to find the right word at just the right moment was unbelievable!

To my lifelong friend, Patti Stirnkorb, for unselfishly editing this book. Your hours of editing are appreciated more than you will ever know.

Caregiver

Individuals who care for another person who cannot care for themselves: Dementia, Alzheimer's, Cancer, Birth Defects, Accident Victim, Stroke, Heart Attack, Surgery, and Other Diseases.

The caregiver is the lifeline for their loved one. They are the voice, advocate, heart, and the able-bodied one, who is all too willing to lend their strength to another in time of need.

This book is written from my perspective as a caregiver for a loved one with dementia. Most, if not all, of these chapters and tips, could be applied to a caregiver with a loved one experiencing a variety of courses, disabilities or illnesses.

BWE

The BWE by my name, on the cover, stands for Best Wife Ever.

I have replaced the word 'widow' with BWE and it is intentional. I am not the only person who qualifies for that title. Any caregiver who gave, or is giving, everything they have to walk their loved one home, has earned more than the widow/widower title. A caregiver's love, attention, compassion, patience, understanding, grace, and mercy has stretched them, and their hearts, more than they ever thought possible. The options include: BWE--Best Wife Ever; BHE--Best Husband Ever; BFR--Best Friend Ever; BSE--Best Sister Ever; BBE--Best Brother Ever: BGE--Best Grandparent Ever, etc.

I love you and respect your contribution to another precious person. God Bless!!

Disclaimer

This book is our family experience and is not intended to cover everything for everyone. Please make personal notes for yourself that apply to your experience.

Caregiver and patients' names have been changed to maintain their privacy.

In reference to legal topics, we acted in accordance with Ohio State and Local laws. Please refer to your own State and Local ordinances for all legal matters.

About the Authors

Anita Yelton is a certified executive coach, facilitator, speaker, trainer with the Maxwell Leadership Team. Anita worked at General Electric(GE) for 31 years.
Anita's domestic and international expertise includes extensive facilitation skills at all levels of the organization; executive coaching/mentoring; individual, team, and organizational development; conflict resolution; and delivery of a variety courses to develop individuals and leaders for the future. She also worked at Medtronic (medical devices) for five years after retiring from GE, where she continued her global teaching, coaching, and speaking.

Jessica McMullin Prior is a young mother of three who is certified in coaching, speaking, and training with the Maxwell Leadership Team.
She spends her time coaching and mentoring single moms and couples who are struggling in their marriage. She has a lifelong love for the written word and is an avid reader which helped immensely with this book. It is important to note she is my granddaughter which made our work together a blessing.

Forward

How did we get here?

I wanted to focus on my purpose: Why I am here on earth? What has God planned for my future? I want to put my God-given purpose into action. In many areas of my life, I've been able to do so. It was in dealing with the caring for, and losing, my beloved husband that I realized I could serve my purpose, even on this journey.

I want to leave a legacy and impact generations. I want to live a life that takes the focus off me and puts it all on others. I want to love like my Savior loves me.

At the age of 75, I thought it is typical to relax, spend time, and 'coast' until God called me home. But, since I am not wired to 'coast', I want to spend my time pouring into others' lives.

Imagine, for a moment: You wake up, get your coffee/tea, and think about your day. Some of you rush off to work, some of you sleep in without "rush" on your mind. Yet, in that same morning, there is another group of people who wake up after only 3-4 hours of sleep. They may not get their coffee for hours—if at all—because they are attending to a loved one that needs their care. Their loved one may or may not even know who they are. They may not be able to communicate or make their needs known. This tired, stressed, and sometimes discouraged, caregiver will move through their day with caution, knowing they might miss something or say the wrong thing, causing a meltdown for the person they love so dearly.

Most people who are caregivers, myself included, were never trained on how to do this 24/7 job. They wish there was training, or help, or both. Most caregivers are in a trial-and-error process which is adding no value to their life, or for that matter, that of their loved one. These people are in desperate need of help, and I feel it is my mission in life to offer that help.

The book you are about to read is intended for caregivers to serve as a guide during a time that may prove difficult to manoeuvre. I have compiled lists in several different categories and have captured my own personal story to share with you-the caregiver-and it is my sincere desire to offer hope and encouragement even through this big, dark, and scary process. There is hope, and I want to help you grab onto it.

Chapter 1

Today: June 29, 2022

Four Months since Tom went to his final home in heaven

It has been 684 days since I started my blog, Dementia Diaries. The writing started from a "nudge" deep inside, when I felt strongly that I was supposed to write a quick, one- time post which has lasted more than two years. We have expanded to include a   bi-weekly Zoom call on Saturday mornings. I have had from zero to six people on our calls. The calls continue, even with low attendance, because God has not released me from this assignment. Even when there has been only one person on the call, I realized I was to minister to that one person who needed to talk.   You can only understand how desperately one needs support unless and until, you are going through something similar.

This book is being written from a caregiver's point of view since I've lived and breathed that role for over five years. We have survived the journey and it was not easy, but God made the journey with us. My son, Ty, and daughter, Tami, have shared this bittersweet endeavor with me. In the last weeks and final days we, and our grandchildren, stayed by his side 24/7.

I take each day one step at a time. Memories and tears flow freely, and I drink it all in as a gift. I have forced myself to have meals with friends, attend a convention in Utah, and take a short vacation with my sister, Gayle. Soon, Gayle and I are taking a trip to Alaska. Tom, Gayle, and I had planned the Alaska trip before the Covid Pandemic hit and the trip was cancelled.

Has it been easy? No. Has it been worth the effort? Yes, priceless!

I hope to provide a caregiver's guide to help you take care of your loved one and yourself. I feel God's presence daily as I pray and talk with Him. When I can't pray, He hears my heart and sees my tears. Life goes on as we adjust to our new reality.

To be a caregiver is to be a family member or helper who regularly looks after a sick, elderly, young, or disabled loved one. It is a selfless, and sometimes draining job. A job made easier when one has a plan—this is what I wish to provide you. My personal memoirs, throughout my endeavors as a caregiver, are written throughout this book.

Come walk with me through our journey.   I'm glad you are here.

The Diagnosis

"Unfortunately, Tom's test results are consistent with Dementia."

I sat back and tried, unsuccessfully, to form words. I was completely stunned. I watched as my daughter leaned in, blinking back tears and doing her best to appear tough for both of us.

The doctor began to speak to us as if Tom wasn't there, as if he were already too far gone to understand. As if the man before him wasn't the very same man who'd built structures, repaired roller coasters, worked on cars, and handled all our finances. The most smart, capable man I knew was being spoken about as if he didn't exist right in front of us.

We left the office in a haze, shock leaving us almost numb to the reality. "I don't want to come back here," Tom almost whispered, his eyes filled with tears.

"You won't have to," I declared, desperately trying to muster confidence for both of us. "I'll take care of you."

Tom was suicidal after that appointment. I chose to go with it, not run from it, as we discussed it almost daily for months. We were reminded of God's promises, and we clung to those like gold. We talked about his desires and end of life decisions, I didn't just listen, I wrote them down and we carried them out.

In the passing days as Tom and I tried to get our feet under us and process his diagnosis, he began to feel intense anger; a hopelessness that made him feel distant from me. He began to tell me that he would not live with this diagnosis; he would end things on his own terms. I couldn't believe it. My travel buddy, my prayer partner, my best friend, wanted to give up and take himself away from our children, grandchildren, great grandchildren, and me.

Quite honestly, it left me at a loss for words, a feeling I don't usually experience. At first. I thought my only course of action was to run away from it! Keep the peace! Maintain the status quo! Luckily a much better option came to me: Go with it.

For the next several months, Tom and I discussed his suicidal thoughts. We trudged through the deepest, darkest depths of him…and at the bottom, we found fear. *Earthshaking, body chilling fear* within a man who felt he was staring death in the face. He was at the threshold of the same disease which took his mother. It was an end of which he was familiar. An end he feared more than life itself; an end he would do anything to escape.

I determined to protect Tom behind the scenes by removing all dangerous weapons from the house. I prayed that God would quickly take Tom's suicidal thoughts from him, which he graciously did.

It's here where I will remind you, beloved caregivers, of the importance of empathy. I couldn't fix Tom's problems. But I could bear witness to his pain. I could remind him of God's promises to us as His children. I could even discuss his end of life wishes and desires. These are conversations held dear to my heart as I laid my love to rest.

Chapter 2

Introduction - Our Story

I met Tom more than 55 years ago. He was my "blind date". My sister was dating his cousin and they invited us to go to Coney Island (Cincinnati) with a group of friends. He was funny and the life of the party. We went and had a great time, with the group. I thought he was "OK" but he didn't live anywhere near me, so I didn't think it would last. We were having a sendoff for him because he was leaving the following week for Vietnam. He asked me to write him while he was gone and promised to write me every day. I laughed inside and I remember thinking two things: 1) I don't write anyone every day and, 2) Ok, I'll do my duty to my country and write to this Army soldier. The End.

The Beginning.... He did write nearly every day and I was shocked that he did what he said he would do. My grandparents lived next door to us, and I would read every single letter to them. I laughed as I read to them thinking he would forget me when he left the Army. I reflected to our Coney Island date, and in addition to him being funny and life of the party, I now thought he was crazy. Crazy because he started saying we were going to get married when he came home. We had one date!

My grandparents thought he was crazy too. I later found out that Tom's grandparents lived up the road from us and my grandmother knew them. She thought highly of them. I knew nothing would come of these letters, but he was in a war, so I kept writing. He surprised me by confessing all his 'faults' in his letters. I did grow to care about him getting home safely, and I prayed for him.

Time flies when you are twenty years old and before I knew it Tom was calling me from Hawaii where he was sent for 'R&R' with the Army: (R&R) Rest & Recuperation (I think). He was getting to leave the war zone for a specific timeframe and then he would go back to war. While in Hawaii he called every day. He let me know he wanted to come to Kentucky when he got out of the Army, and drive me to Georgia to meet his parents. Also, he wanted us to get married ASAP. I wondered what he was drinking, (just kidding). But his sincerity quickly won me over. It wasn't long before I was daydreaming of a fluffy white dress and a beautiful winter wedding.

Long story short, he came back to the states in September of that year. My mother actually let me ride to Atlanta with him for a week to meet his parents, brother, and sister. My grandmother, knowing his grandmother, convinced my mother to let me go. We had to call my mother as soon as we arrived, and we were not to be alone during that week. Tom's parents picked up the gauntlet and stayed with us every day until he drove me home. Tom called me at Thanksgiving and asked me to marry him after Christmas. I must have been crazy because I said yes.

We married December 30, 1967. And as they say, the rest is history.

We celebrated 54 years of marriage the December before I lost Tom. He didn't remember much of our past. I remember all of our time together, more than half a century. I remember both good and bad and reminded him of some events every day. Now, I keep those stories safe and sound in my heart for the both of us. Being able to be on the Dementia journey with Tom was…priceless.

And there we were, living every day like it was new, because to Tom, it was. He had no memory of any of the snapshots of our story that I shared with him; no beloved friends, no hardships, no breathe-deep moments, not even our children or grandchildren. I was the only person he knew on sight, and I prepared myself for the day when that memory was gone as well.

Planning ahead is great for vacation or going to the grocery, but **critical** when you are a caregiver. Lack of planning can result in an outcome that causes loss or pain. I believe it is critical to have a family meeting early on to update them and come up with a gameplan. Decide who is the main contact, how much assistance (emotional, financial, personal, time) is needed. Decide who to tell and when you will tell them. Denial is your enemy.

It is extremely important to talk openly about the disease and how it will progress; end of life care decisions must be made. You want loved one to have input as to what he/she wants. Because Tom was suicidal in the early stage, having him involved in decisions was critical. I was then able to reassure him that I would honor his wishes as long as I was physically able. He died comfortably at home.

I put together a Planning Blueprint for myself and added, deleted, and changed it as needed. This is something I'd like to share with you. This is meant as a guide, a template of sorts, to help you get started on your own plan.

Chapter 3

Planning Blueprint

This is a list of precautionary, and necessary, items that should be incorporated into your plan. These have been added to as we realized, by experience, what was needed to make sure we were prepared for any situation.

A) Have a fireproof/waterproof folder or box for:

- Medical cards
- Vaccine cards
- List of Medications with dosage, how many times a day, and what time of day they should be taken
- Social Security Card
- Driver's License or State ID
- Legal paperwork, Power of Attorney and an up-to-date will
  - Make sure the will is up-to-date with one or more of the children, and/or a substitute, listed on it to make medical and financial decisions

B) Caregiver Bag for a Hospital or Emergency room visit (to grab quickly):

- Phone and charger
- iPad/tablet/computer, iWatch and charger
- Your medication (if any) and loved one's medicine (or list mentioned above)
- Extension cord, paper & pens, reading glasses
- Bible and other reading material

C) Items for Home Use

- Baby monitor/camera, baby wipes, chux pads - (Disposable and washable)
- Disposable gloves
- Large, glow in the dark house number on home or mailbox (for emergency vehicles to see easily)
- Antibacterial soap and disinfectant wipes
- Rinse free hair and bath sponges or wipes (by Scrubzz)
- Phone numbers for doctors secured to the refrigerator
- List of bills that need to be paid
- Passwords for credit cards, e-bill pay, phone, computer, etc.
- Pill Holder
- Silicone placemat for table (by Upward Baby)
- First Aid Kit
- Pill container and pill splitter
- Waterproof mattress pad
- Disposable leak proof pads

D) Medical Bag for home use

- Blood pressure cuff and batteries
- Thermometer
- Kardia heart monitor (use with phone) (Amazon)
- Pulse Oximeter to measure oxygen levels (finger)

E) Trunk/car Emergency Bag

- Diapers/Pull Ups/clean underwear

- Baby wipes, disinfectant wipes, rinse free wash clothes, paper towels, chux pads, disposal gloves, plastic bags (for wet clothes)
- Change of clothes: shirt, pants, socks, undershirt, shoes, towel, bottle of water (don't ask me why I know this)

F) The business of death, have copies of:

- Social Security Card
- Birth certificate
- Marriage License (if applicable)
- Military ID and DD214
- State ID or Driver's License

G) Helpful hints

- Notify pharmacist of who has permission to pick up prescriptions (more than one person is helpful)
- Notify family doctor who to contact; loved one must sign authorization form, do this early in the diagnosis.

Chapter 4

Where Do You Start?

It's hard to know what to do when it starts. You notice the memory is slowly changing. The same questions are repeated over and over. Is this normal memory loss associated with the aging process? Is it stress? Or am I imagining it? In our case it took a year to make an appointment with a Neurologist to rule out Alzheimer's that plagued Tom's mother, and my grandmother.

Tom's diagnosis felt to me, what I imagined it would feel like, to be the trainer at sea world who was crushed by a killer whale. I was absolutely flattened, and the only thing holding me together was a wetsuit of faith and my family. Caregivers, the diagnosis is going to awaken every negative emotion you've ever felt; anger, depression, fear, anxiety, just to name a few. I can't express how important it is to find a support group that you can lean on, and trust, to carry these emotions with you. They're heavy and not meant to be hauled alone.

As you're dealing with your feelings associated with this horrid disease, remember that your loved one is also impacted. They may not show it. They may seem to be only angry or explosive. But underneath the external emotions will be raw fear and grief over losing their memories, their freedom, their very selves. Do your best to be a sounding board from which they can draw support, and a soft place to fall. Remember that it takes emotional support in order to be someone else's emotional support. Make sure that you have a sounding board as well.

For some reason I felt that when the official diagnosis was made there were things we needed to do quickly to protect our family. I felt we needed to talk to a lawyer right away to make sure we knew all the legal aspects of Dementia. The first thing he recommended was to draw up a Power of Attorney (POA) for our daughter and myself to act in all matters related to medical and financial issues. The paperwork was drawn up within a couple of days. Tom, Tami, and I signed the POA, and it became an official document.

Once the POA was signed we took it to our doctor to have it scanned into our medical records. Within our first six-eight months we took the POA to our bank, credit union, our accountant, our creditors, and pharmacy.   The difficult discussion was the driver's license and the actual driving. Since it was early in Tom's diagnosis we waited and watched his driving habits. He did well for about another six months and then we had a big decision to make: He needed to stop driving.

The decision was taken out of our hands when he totaled his truck at the end of our driveway. Yes, in sight of our home. Our house is back off the main street about 1000 feet and he was on his way home and hit a parked truck on the main street. Most of the damage was on the passenger side of the truck and Tom only had minor injuries. That was "Decision Day"; he could no longer drive a vehicle. I could only imagine what that news did to him. I thought about how I would feel if that privilege was taken away from me, resulting in yet another loss of independence. I believe it is one of the biggest freedoms that actually defines us as individuals when we reach adulthood. When that right is taken away, one can feel as though they're less of a person.

We realized when the diagnosis of Dementia was made, that the day would arrive. If Tom were in an accident where others were injured, it would have been his fault, no matter what. Once the Dementia diagnosis was known, it was up to us, his family, to make the determination of when to stop allowing him to drive.   The next day our family doctor told Tom he could no longer drive. I asked the doctor to tell him so I could always blame the doctor when Tom got mad at me.

To add to Tom's indignance, there were times when he'd forgotten he couldn't drive adding to his frustration. It was then that I had to remind him. The state ID did make him feel better, but it took about a year to get to a place where Tom stopped asking to drive, and blaming me. It was something I could live with because others' lives were at stake. Tom's despair was evident at this time, and he began to voice thoughts of harming himself. Tom was despondent, and I worried that he might act on his self-harming thoughts. He told the kids and I that he would living with Dementia was not something he wanted to put our family through. But somehow we made it through those tough days.

Chapter 5

The Toughest Conversation

As mentioned before, I decided to have an honest conversation with Tom about his wishes as the disease progressed. I told him that I wanted to know his thoughts so I could use that information as we had to make decisions along the way. From that point on, we talked about Dementia frequently.

It was at this time that I made him a promise: "I will keep you at home for as long as I can physically take care of you." That promise guided all of our decisions as a family from then on. It took the burden off my shoulders enabling me to remind him about that promise from time to time. It helped to ease his anxiety.

The first full year flew by as Tom was only in the early stages of Dementia. It didn't require much on my part, except to listen to him talk about his job and Vietnam a hundred times. In fact, I heard it so often I could have done a 'lip sync' on both topics. Initially I wanted to scream, but in the later stages of his Dementia as he quit talking, I would have loved to hear him tell his stores one more time.

If I've said it once, I'll say it one hundred more times; please, my dear caregiver, give yourself permission to be frustrated. This disease carries with it an enormous amount of grief, anxiety, and depression. We are each entitled to those feelings. We are losing a pillar of our life just as they are losing us. To add insult to injury, they are still standing in front of us with the invisible barrier of dementia still somehow separating us from one another. It happens agonizingly slow. Give yourself space to feel, process, and voice your emotions so that they cannot steal your power. Find a way to vent your frustrations constructively, whether it be through journaling or a trusted confidant. Remember, denial is your enemy. It is especially your enemy when you're denying yourself the space to feel without self-judgement.

It was about this time that I started a list of things that we needed to do early in the Dementia process. I'm a list maker and must write things down. This list has been edited, changed, and worked on over time to share with other caregivers. This list helped me to be able to live with my decisions and have no regrets.

Chapter 6

Things To Do Early in Diagnosis (Pt. 1)

"Do what you can live with, and have no regrets"

As the famous missionary Jim Elliot once said, "when it comes time to die, make sure that is all you have to do."

I still remember my beloved pastor reading this beautiful quote at Tom's funeral. I remember seeing the vessel that carried my sweetheart, lying not 10 feet in front of me. I remember the smell of flowers; a smell I always adored but now carried a hollow ache within my chest every time I drew a breath. I remember the gasping sobs of my daughter, the somber face of my son, and the hands of all six of my grandchildren reaching up to comfort me at various times.

As my pastor read this quote, he said "Tom was ready to die. He had some notice, many do not. Tom's death was a process, but his difficult journey was never taken alone. He was surrounded by his family that loved him, and his beautiful wife, Anita," I remember the only thought that shattered its way through the fog of my own disbelief, was the thought that I would never again on this side of heaven, hear my best friend call me beautiful. Such a mundane, ordinary phrase that the sting of its absence is often underplayed. I began to let my mind wander to our early marriage and parenthood. Tom and I had made mistakes, some grievous and some miniscule. But Tom lived his life with no regrets. "It is what it is until it ain't" he'd chirp. The slight twang of his southern accent always brought me such comfort and stability. I couldn't believe I'd never hear that voice again until joining him in our heavenly home.

I realized that, like Tom, I had no regrets. I'd discussed Tom's death; I knew exactly what he wanted for his funeral and executed it with ease and a peace that only a resolution made between lovers can give. I'd honored my love in life and in death, not perfectly but I'd "done what I could live with." The simplicity of this phase—I acknowledged with a smile—would have made it an everyday euphemism for Tom. Oh, how he loved to share those plain old nuggets of wisdom with anyone who would listen!

It is here, caregiver, that I give you a message that only one on the other side of grief could utter: Protect your family. Protect yourself. Gift yourself with the time to grieve later, by trudging through as much clerical work as you possibly can now. Not only will the process be much harder after your loved one has passed, but it will also pull you away from the process of your grief unnecessarily and frequently. Protect yourself and your family from jumping through hoops as you try to process the absence. Avoid mistakes by not taking all the steps needed to get your affairs in order. I am happy to say that I followed this list myself. In the days before and after the funeral, I had only to love on my tribe, as we started this well-weathered, but dreaded journey called grief, together.

- Journal your journey. Putting your thoughts on paper will help you as you write and will be a historical record for you and your family
- Have an attorney create a Power of Attorney for finances and health decisions
- Have a backup plan. Another family member, a friend, or another caregiver that you can call on when you need help, need to talk, or in an emergency
- Talk to him/her about their wishes and what they want done
- Don't make promises you can't keep

- Write down all their passwords, accounts, bills, budget, insurance details, prescriptions, doctor names & phone numbers, church contacts, important medical information
- Get your name added to all accounts, banking (checking, savings, IRA)
- Have the doctor document the diagnosis and give you a dated copy
- Do not let insurance lapse (life, health, etc.)
- Carry their driver's license, military ID, insurance, Covid-19 shots, list of medications, state ID, etc. Keep the originals and give them a color copy
- Have phone numbers to reach palliative care and Hospice
- Have a silicone bracelet with diagnosis and contact information (Dementia, their name, please call (your name) (your phone number). Once they start wearing it, do not draw attention to it, or take it off
- When driving becomes an issue, keep keys to car where they can't find them (or give the extra key to your back up person)
- Have the doctor tell them they can no longer drive and get a state ID to replace their driver's license
- Keep all medications out of reach Give medication as scheduled
- Remove or hide dangerous items from your home (guns, knives, box cutter, scissors)

Chapter 7

Things to Do Early in Diagnosis (Pt.2)

Family Meeting

When this topic comes to mind, I always picture an escape room. Places designed to create an artificially stressful situation where groups of friends, family, or even coworkers' mutual objective, is to find a way to escape the situation. In a way, life in general is an escape room. We are all just working toward the end goal of being with our Heavenly Father in paradise.

Escape rooms have a way of bringing out the fundamental differences of the people around us. One person may handle crisis well, and thus take it as their own personal responsibility to complete the task with zero assistance. One person may bark orders to everyone else, unable to mobilize their own bodies but still able to delegate tasks. Another person may shut down completely and find themselves totally unsure of what to say or do.

When a loved one is diagnosed with a terminal illness, it can feel like you and all those around you, have been locked into a permanent escape room. One where the only objective is to safely walk your loved one home as a team.

It is important to remember that being a part of the caregiving "team" is a choice. You will have family members who are willing to participate heavily, ones who are willing to lend a hand here and there, and others who—for one reason or another—just don't have help to give.

It benefits any team to have a game plan going into a situation. When it comes to "team caregiver", the best way to make this happen is a family meeting.

Some families may tend to ignore or put off a meeting of the minds for various reasons. It could be conflict between a few members; it could be grief over the situation; it could even be them wishing the situation away completely, and not wanting to acknowledge it by speaking of it. Regardless, the desire to avoid a family meeting must be overcome. Denial is your enemy and time is of the essence!

A family should represent love, compassion, safety, and unity. Unfortunately, this is not the case for all families. Some families have different dynamics, such as violence, vengeance, hate, abuse of many different natures, and more. These families are not able to come together as a unit when problems and health issues arise because they are blocked by negativity and toxicity. They need help as much as other families, but sometimes a simple facilitator or mediator cannot offer the type of help they require. There are times when a situation is so inflamed, that only a professional can step in and de-escalate things. If you are in a family like this, it may be prudent to come up with a back up plan that might not include family at all.

In situations with lesser or no conflict, a neutral facilitator—someone with no vested interest in the outcome—can be used to help a family come together and make important decisions. I have added a few reference sheets/lists to guide facilitators in helping families during these meetings.

Facilitator's Step-By-Step Guide

This is an outline, a basic template that you can use. You might tweak it, change or eliminate items, or add things you feel necessary. Just make sure, if your family needs this step, that you do it. This is assuming that a third-party person is the facilitator, mediator or pastor—not the primary caregiver.

1. Date and Attendees
2. Meeting Guidelines
   - Assume a positive intent
   - Full participation
   - One conversation at a time
   - Confidentiality
   - Active listening (eyes, ears, heart)
   - Ask questions
   - Maintain an open mind
3. Roles
   - Timekeeper
   - Progress checker (are we following our meeting guidelines?)
   - Facilitator
   - Scribe (action items, parking lot issues, and agreements)
4. Discuss the purpose of this meeting
5. Discuss the expectations
6. Discuss the boundaries and Non-Negotiables
7. Capture the action items (agreements written down)
8. Capture the parking lot issues
9. Capture loved one's wishes (if present or for later discussion)
10. Decisions: Caregiver, home care or facility, work or quit, finances, etc.

Talk About Their Childhood, Early Years, School/College, Military Service

Sharing stories of how, where, when, and why we are who we are, is a great way to prepare for future conversations. Make a mental and written list of a few stock questions that can easily be asked several times in one afternoon. These will prove quite useful for children, grandchildren, or any other visiting family who finds themselves tongue tied at the prospect of conversing with our declining loved one. This was very helpful to me when Tom's Dementia reached a point where he no longer remembered current events, family members, etc.

Being able to talk to him about his past was a great way to communicate because that's what he remembered. It also stimulated his brain when I asked him about living on Christmas Lane, being in Vietnam, or other events from his past. I wanted to keep him communicating as long as possible.

Questions are the best way to get your loved one to talking as they decline and revert back to their early years. Sample questions I used include:

- What sports did you play as a kid? Did you enjoy it?
- What were your favorite activities when you were younger?
- Who were your best friends? What did you do when with them?
- What church, high school, college did you attend?
- Tell us your funniest childhood memory? Best and worst memory?
- Did you eat dinner as a family? What was a typical dinner like?
- Tell me about your brothers/sisters.
- Were you in the military? What branch? Where did you serve?
- Did you live in a big city or the suburbs?
- What did you do for work? Did you like it?

- Where did you meet your spouse?
- Note: Ask open ended questions that require more than a yes or no reply.
- Add follow up questions after they answer.

Chapter 8

Preparing Your Home

There is really no way of knowing all the things needed to prepare your home for this unknown journey. I put all the information I could think of into a small black notebook. I kept the black book in a secure place where it could not be easily found.

The following list is a copy of the final list that I compiled hoping it would be useful to other caregivers.

- My **little black book** – start putting important information in one place and keep it in a safe place. Let trusted family members know where they can access this information if needed
  - Passwords to anything that's password protected
  - Where valuables are located
  - Insurance companies and policy numbers
  - Credit Cards and relevant account information
  - Important names, phone numbers and why they are important
  - Utility names and account numbers
  - Investment institutions and account numbers
  - Instructions, how and when bills are to be paid (checks, automatic payments, e-pay, etc.
  - Combination to safe (if you have one; consider investing in one if you do not)
  - Contributions to pay
  - Titles to vehicles, home, camper, etc. Make sure they are all titled

- Apple/Google ID's, login, and passwords
- Designate personal items and to whom they are to be given
- Be ready to put plastic isle runners in your hallway when they can no longer hold their bladder; remove carpet and replace with wood or linoleum- if carpet gets ruined
- Have hand sanitizer in every room next to antibacterial soap
- Don't rearrange furniture as it causes confusion
- Be ready to take over finances, paying bills, taking out trash and recyclables, appointments, paying taxes and filing them
- Keep an eye on him/her with pets and children
- Install small night lights throughout the house
- Install a baby gate at the top of stairs
- Identify and correct potential fall hazards
- Ensure all banking accounts have beneficiaries listed and on record
- Get a Durable Power of Attorney (POA) to make legal and medical decisions when your loved one can no longer make decisions Note: once the patient passes, the POA is no longer valid
- Keep the living will up-to-date and ensure you have someone to make medical and financial decisions for you in the event of illness or death
- Funeral planning: Allow your loved one to say exactly what they want regarding final arrangements, disposal of their body, the funeral services, etc.
- Transfer on Death (POA) the deed to your home, if you own it. Fill out and file with your county. When death happens, take ID, and death certificate to the county building and the deed is signed over

Helpful hints

- Remove weapons from the home (guns, knives, etc.)
- Hide Medications in a safe place, out of site
- Hide extra car keys or give to a trusted person

Chapter 9

Caregiver Concerns and Worries

The list of concerns and worries is long, but not complete. I have felt most of these, but not all of them. Each of these can come and go quickly and some may linger. These things are real and typically kept inside, whether consciously or unconsciously. An outsider can't see beyond your smile or claims to be 'fine' if they ask how you are doing.

As a caregiver it is so important to do a self-assessment from time to time. It's important to do a reality check on how *you* are doing. An honest assessment can help you identify what's working and what's not working, as well as actions that you need to take. Don't be afraid to ask for help.

These actions could include things like getting counseling, talking to a friend or another caregiver, sincerely praying about it, talking to your pastor, journaling your feelings, joining a support group, exercising, planning your days, reading a book, setting aside quality time with your loved one, writing a book, working in the garden, projects around your house, having friends stop by for short visits, etc.

Some of the things on the list may need to be discussed with your personal doctor and/or treated with medication. Please do not hesitate to talk to your doctor.

I have two close family members who both struggle with anxiety and depression. Each had issues and finally tired of hiding it and keeping it inside, sought professional help. Pride often keeps us from seeking help, but please remember that you are valid, and you are worth fighting for.

Below is a list of common stressors caregivers may confront. These are often things that have no real solution, but can be better coped with, if acknowledged. Perhaps through journaling or discussing it with those around you, stress can be alleviated or lessened.

- Your personal health
- Regret
- No one to talk to
- Loneliness
- Frequent changes
- Sadness
- Loss of friends
- Your personal safety
- Loved one getting lost
- Slower pace
- No adult conversation
- Missing your spouse (even while they are sitting next to them)
- Losing things
- Money (how do we pay for things? Can we even afford to be sick?)
- Self-pity
- Depression and anxiety as disease progresses
- Shame over losing your temper
- Embarrassment at how you handled stress in front of your loved one
- Anger—why us? Why am I stuck thinking for two people?
- Scared of the future
- Mood Swings: Coping with them for both caregiver and loved one

- Lack of sleep
- Fatigue
- No personal time
- No quiet time
- Emotional roller coaster that is dementia
- Engaging or walking away
- Guilt for what I said or did

Chapter 10

Suggested Activities

to Do with Your Loved One

Taking your loved one out of the house while they are still able can be fun and create lasting memories. It is imperative that you plan these activities. People with dementia can often become overstimulated, and activities that are all day or crowded, are inadvisable. Depending on the stage of the disease, it may also be wise to pack some snacks, drinks to keep them hydrated, a change of clothes as well as disposable underwear and sanitary wipes. Think of this as your "grown up diaper bag." Take lots of pictures because you will cherish them later in your journey.

Since no one can predict how long he or she will live, we need to consider that we, the caregivers, could "go home" first. That means the activities, pictures and memories could comfort your family and loved one when you are gone. Make sure to have a back up caregiving plan in the event that this happens.

Activities also provide closeness and give you a break from the daily routines, worries, and stressors.

- Go to a local park to sit or walk, or both
- Get ice cream, shop, and enjoy your favorite flavor
- Visit the Zoo and the children's zoo where you can pet the animals
- Visit the Ark and other local attractions
- Indoor mall walking
- Grocery store

- Join the YMCA close to your home
- Join the local senior center
- Train ride
- Veterans Administration (VA)
- Putt-Putt
- Ceramics
- Exercise
- Write a story of your memories with them
- Play with kids
- Listen to music
- Help them call a friend or relative
- Watch TV
- Gardening, plant/cut flowers,
- Games (kids) and puzzles
- Card games
- Do dishes together
- Cook together
- Go to any local "hot" spots. Tom loved a trip to Ikea or Jungle Jim's
- Painting, adult/kid's coloring books and crayons
- Look at old photos and ask them to identify the people or events
- Draw or learn to draw
- Play I Spy
- Go out to eat, sit outside at the café and watch people going by
- Take pictures with your phone or their phone (selfies too)

Chapter 11

General Tips for Caregivers

As a caregiver, I have learned these tips through experience, pain, laughter, and sadness for myself, as well as Tom. Early on in my journey, I would never have dreamed how many times I'd lament that I didn't have a survival guide. I struggled so you don't have to! There may be tips you don't use, or additional ones you come up with through trial and error. Pay it forward to the next caregiver you meet and provide them with your own survival tips—or better yet, this book!

Keeping track of the tips I found particularly useful was extremely helpful to me. Doing so actually helped create the tips I am bestowing on you.

These examples were not always gained without making mistakes and learning from them. It also required some apologies on my part. I encourage you to never hesitate to apologize or say something that was hurtful to your loved one. It's always a fine line that we walk as caregivers, and the apologies are for both people in this journey.

- As difficult as it is for you, it is often more difficult for them
- You will go through multiple emotions over and over
- Highs and lows come with no warning
- Your loved one can't reason or choose their responses
- You are only human and will have human reactions & worries
- Don't be too hard on yourself
- It is good to be quick to listen and slow to talk

- The silence can be harder than repeating everything
- Ask them to help you with simple projects as long as possible
- Use the past to your advantage. Remember the simple things, the funny things that brought life, joy, fun, humor, laughter to your life and use them over and over because it's only a 'repeat' to you and it is new them every time
- As your loved one will go through different Dementia phases/stages determine a mental "age" where they seem to be speaking from and then speaking to them with age-appropriate responses and questions
- Redirecting your loved one from negative thoughts or actions to a more positive direction. Redirecting your loved one is a gift, use it because it is a valuable tool
- Encourage them; try not to talk down to them
- There are moments of clarity, and it will be a treasure for you. Remember to breathe those moments deeply as they will become increasingly fleeting
- Keep hope alive; seek help if you feel you are losing hope
- Simple things will become difficult to them; try to be patient
- An incredibly difficult thing is when your loved one inevitably must stop driving; be aware of that time.
  -Suggestion: ask your doctor to break the news to your loved one that they can no longer drive. They may accept it easier. Even if they are mad…they are not mad at you
- Reinforce your love for them, and tell them often
- Don't say "you can't" rather have them do what they can, use words like "would you like to…."
- Physical touch is a gift from you to show your loved one that they are still loved
- Join a support group
- Journal your days/weeks/months

- Use color bowls and plates instead of white so they can see their food (vision and hearing can decline as they do)
- A raised toilet seat with handles can be installed over the existing toilet seat to aid them in getting up and down
- Agree, don't argue
- Ask, don't demand
- Keep a fireproof and waterproof bag (Doc Fortress) for important papers such as: Legal paperwork, medical cards (copies), vaccine cards, passports, list of all medication, Power of Attorney (POA), driver's license or state ID, military ID and DD214, social security card, marriage license, death certificate so that you can grab it to go to the attorney, the hospital, etc.
- Don't interrupt when they are talking
- Sit and eat with them- companionship is important!
- Never shame them; distract them from what they are doing
- Use active listening; listen to understand not just to respond
- Play their favorite music
- Reassure; don't lecture
- Don't assume Dementia without a diagnosis as it could be normal aging memory loss
- Repeat kindly, don't say "I told you"
- Use "and" instead of "but" example: a) we could go but... vs. b) we could go and...

I know that this list may appear staggering to the new caregiver who has just begun their journey. It is important to remember that you won't have to master each of these points at once. They are all from various stages of the disease as it progresses. You will most likely not master all of these points right away; you will probably fail, as I have, daily. When you feel self-conscious or guilt stricken, please remember that our heavenly Father forgives us if we stumble, and we must forgive ourselves so that we can move forward. This list for you is from lessons I have learned. You may not need all of them and feel free to add to the list for yourself.

Chapter 12

Lessons Learned Early

Dementia, much like parenting, does not come with a manual. I still remember all the ways I thought I'd do better than my already excellent mother, and the mothers before her, and the mothers before that….

It didn't take long for reality, dirty diapers, and the wails of my once adorable and charming little ones transitioned into toddlers. Once I'd finally thought I'd gotten the whole toddler thing down, my little ones morphed, seemingly overnight, into these creative, smart, kind, sometimes wild, full-grown KIDS. To add a little bit of extra spice to life, just as my Tami was starting kindergarten, Tom was in a major motorcycle collision.

On that fateful day which would turn our little growing family completely on its axis, my phone rang. Such a usual upbeat sound would forever cause a minor amount of anxiety inside of my heart after this day.

"Hello," I answered cheerfully, ignorant of the trauma that awaited me on the other end.

"Mrs. Yelton?" Inquired a nervous voice.

"Yes?"

"Hello, this is Tom's supervisor at Kings Island. We're calling to let you know that your husband was in an accident—oh! Could you hold on a second?"

The silence rang out for five agonizing minutes, which I now look back with an almost stunned sort of humor that any rational person would actually alert a wife to an accident and then leave her in suspense as to the state of her husband. Shortly after, I was told with little more explanation than I was given at the beginning of the phone call, that it was better I come to Bethesda North Hospital as soon as possible and see for myself. A gracious neighbor took Ty and Tami to her house, and I rushed to the hospital, a knot of anxiety and fear forming in the pit of my stomach.

When I arrived, I was told that Tom would lose his legs and they were too damaged to even try to operate. Tom was never one to be told what to do, and he wasn't about to start accepting orders from others now. Out of spite, he not only healed enough to keep his legs but also learned to walk despite being told he'd be wheelchair bound for the rest of his life. He lived with the scars from that point on and was in debilitating pain for most of his life, but he didn't let that block his path from doing whatever he wanted. His gutsy spirit was one I'd always envied. It wasn't until our dementia journey began that I realized all those years watching him be the bravest person I knew, had rubbed off on me. Like Tom, we all live with the scars of our mistakes.

They're inevitable. We're imperfect people who serve a perfect God and we have no control over our shortcomings. What we do have sovereignty over, is what we do with our mistakes. For me, I decided to list a few lessons I learned from trial and error and from some bursts of God-given wisdom. My hope is that you will read this list and instead of duplicating my mistakes, you will make shiny, brand-new ones of your own! The beauty of messing up is that our heavenly Father waits in the wings to forgive us as soon as they happen, and He uses them to drive us into a deeper closeness and dependence on Him.

Feel free to add to this list and all the lists included in this book, so that you can share them with others to help them in their journey.

- No two days are the same

- As they decline, give them fewer choices, example would be do you want this or that instead of "what do you want to eat"
- When they start putting on different clothes all day, or take them all out of the closet, limit the number of clothes and shoes in the closet
- Give them tasks and small jobs to help them feel needed and useful
- Prayer and church were critical to both of us, and Tom was able to attend church up until three weeks before his death
- Music, music, music, and some dancing
- Loneliness, lack of sleep, no rest, and no one to talk to are normal stressors
- Dementia impacts the individual, family, and friends
- Our non-verbal expressions need to be positive and in sync with our words. Smile as often as possible
- Treat them with dignity and respect at all times, they hate the disease as much as you do, if not more
- The journey is an emotional roller coaster for the patient and the caregiver
- They like routine and things where they are supposed to be, after they move it, return it to its appropriate location
- They bring you gifts, and sometimes they are your things
- Profanity is a choice we make every day to use or not to use, they can lose their ability to choose because their filters are gone
- Face to face conversation is preferred over phone conversation
- Show love, mercy, grace, and compassion everyday

- Self-reflection is critical: motives, intentions, and actions that I did or didn't do
- It's okay to not be okay, but it is not okay to take it out on them
- Think before you speak because words can confuse them
- Changes can take hours, days, months or may not happen at all
- Don't go to bed angry at them or with them
- Do what you can live with and have no regrets

Chapter 13

Conversation Starters

Tom had two siblings he loved very much: Kenna and Tim. Being that he was so much older than Kenna, Tom's love for Kenna resembled more of a fatherly affection than that of a brother and sister. As for Tim—he was Tom's very own live-in best friend for their entire childhood. They remained just as close event though they lived 8-hours apart for most of their adult lives.

One of the last times Tim came to visit Tom was one of the most bittersweet things a person can witness. I remember Tim walking in the door and the puzzled look on Tom's face. He scrutinized every inch of Tim's features, confusion turning to desperation. Tears began to fill his eyes as Tom rushed forward in one swift motion to hug his brother. He didn't let go for what felt like hours, clinging to Tim as if clinging to a life float, rescuing himself from drowning surrounded by ever-crashing waves. There was not a dry eye in the room as I watched the brothers wrap their arms around each other in a way that could only be experienced by deeply connected souls.

When the embrace ended, I could tell by Tom's expression that while his memory was not able to recognize the man before him. The same man whom he had just squeezed, with what seemed to be all of his strength for such a long time, his soul—the very depths of my Tom's spirit where the real him had been hidden away by his disease, knew without a shadow of a doubt that this man was a person he deeply loved. A person he knew better than he'd known himself at one point in life. A person he trusted, a person he admired, a person he would forever be willing to lay down his life.

Kenna's visit was much different than Tim's, but equally as gut wrenching. Before she'd arrived to visit Tom, Kenna was well aware that he may not remember her. I think that fact is something that can easily be understood intellectually, but which you can never be prepared… Kenna watched as Tom's blank face stared back at her. I could see lines of worry between her brows, her eyes widening in a way that a character in a horror movie would look, realizing that a person they loved had been dragged under the depths by the Loch Ness monster. Tom may have been standing before Kenna, a living breathing person who looked just like her brother, but her beloved protector was no more. As far as she could see, that person was taken long ago, and the one who stood in his place simply did not know her.

Kenna, being full of the fire her mother had passed onto her, and to Tom, refused to allow her visit to be for nothing. "Okay, well then you need to teach me how to talk to my brother," she had declared to me the very moment we were alone.

And talk she did! Kenna—one who is uniquely gifted to pull conversation out of anyone, (maybe even animals), walked Tom up and all along the length of our property. She asked him a large array of questions to which she already knew all the answers. She told him stories he'd heard a thousand times over, she told him about her house that he'd visited years before but wouldn't be able to recall by now. She even talked about how much she loved him. Tom may not have been able to grasp that concept as he was, but he did know that he liked this lady who walked with him and made conversation.

Learning from Kenna's stubborn act of love, and the role I had played in equipping her with the right questions to ask, I created a 3x5 card with a few topics for those who wanted to talk to Tom. This allowed others to utilize topics in order to connect with him. I shared them with people with whom we went to dinner. I shared them with church members who'd sat a row away from us for the better part of 3 decades. I shared them with my grandchildren. I even shared them with Tom's nurses when the home visits began. I also carried a 3x5 card in my wallet to show waiters, waitresses, doctors, shop owners, etc. It read, "My husband, Tom has dementia, and he may not be able to respond to you very well. Feel free to ask me as I will be paying. Thank you for making him comfortable." These cards were my own little way of gifting my husband with the dignity I desired for him. He deserved that much from the people around him as his world began to shrink.

Another source of inspiration for the cards was watching Tom's confused face, as long held acquaintances greeted him in a familiar way. He could only manage a weak "Hey Guy" or "Hi Lady." I admit, it was a wonder to me that Tom never lost his cheerful demeanor when he greeted people. He may not have known who they were, but he still wanted to brighten their day. No one ever embarrassed him by pointing out that he'd forgotten their names, and for that, I'm so thankful. God answered my prayers.

These conversation starters are intended for two specific situations. 1) To give you a variety of topics to help when you tire of the same conversations every day, and 2) to share with family, friends or volunteers who sit with your loved one, giving you time away from home.

- Tell me about yourself
- Where did you grow up?
- How did you meet your husband, wife, significant other?
- How many children do you have?
- How many kids, grandkids, great grandkids do you have?
- Do they live nearby?
- What do you like to read?
- Where do you like to walk?
- What kind of music do you like?
- Do you like to sing?

- Do you like to dance?
- Do you like to travel? Where have you trave

- led? Where was your favorite place to visit? Why?
- Do you have pets? What are they? What are their names?
- Would you like for me to read to you? What book?
- Do you play a musical instrument? Can you play something for me?
- Did you serve in the military? What branch? Where did you serve?
- Would you like to help me put a puzzle together?

It is important to always keep in mind that dementia can quickly deteriorate conversational skills, and there will come a time when these questions don't work. At that point, their answers have been forgotten. Once that time arrives, it is imperative that a shift is made from conversation to companionship. Read a book, sing songs to them, turn on a movie and talk to them about the events transpiring in the film. Anything to keep from too much silence. As dementia causes those whom we love to get quieter and quieter, it is common to think that they will desire quiet, but usually the opposite is true. A few kind words can remind our loved ones that we are here, they are not alone, and they are cared for deeply.

Chapter 14

Key Phrases

Two months after Tom was called home, our granddaughter, Jessi woke up on a warm spring morning and fell to the floor. Her legs had stopped functioning. She was rushed to the hospital, as we all hoped and prayed the problem would be quickly resolved, or even curable.

Jessi was admitted and transported to a better equipped hospital where she endured brain scans, MRI's of almost every part of her body, a spinal tap, and many other painful and invasive procedures. Jessi had taken Tom's death particularly hard and was prone to poor mental health at times, so the Memah inside me wanted to visit my girl who reminded me so much of myself in so many ways.

I looked at her sleeping form, seemingly crumbled weakly in her hospital bed, and whispered a few prayers, waiting for her to wake up so I could see for myself how she was doing. That day, we played cards and joked and laughed and I remember thinking she was doing really well, handling it better than most people twice her age would be with this situation.

It was only a few days later that I came to visit Jessi and found her in a completely different state. I was greeted by the red face of a sobbing young wife and mom who seemed to feel devoid of all hope.

"I'm so angry with God!" she lamented, her voice breaking as it did when she was small and desperately needing comfort. "First he took my Popah—my very first best friend-- away from me, and then he took my legs too!" Her heaving sobs filled the room, leaving me at a loss of what to do.

"Memah," she quivered. "What if I'm like this forever? What if I never heal? What if I never walk? What if I can't run with my babies or dance with my husband?"

I took a deep breath, summoning wisdom from a lesson I'd learned long ago that barely related to the current issue. Nonetheless, what my Jessi was facing prompted me to say, "Jessi, remember when Popah was so angry all the time and we worried about him never coming out of his rage and bitterness?"

She frowned deeply. "Yeah, I do. But you weren't even worried back then. Why are you telling me this?" she sniffed expectantly.

"I was worried. I'm just a Memah who didn't want to burden my granddaughter. Those were worries of a woman in a phase of life that you won't reach for many decades." I closed my eyes and prayed that God would allow this lesson to speak to her and not deepen her despair at the mention of her Popah. "Honey, I had to stop questioning 'what if' about your Popah. It was a waste of what little time I had left with him on this earth. I had to replace my 'what ifs' with 'EVEN ifs'. I had to trust that EVEN IF God did not take the current struggle from us, He would use it for His honor and glory, and that He would hold me and our family in the palm of His hand."

Months later, it was discovered that Jessi suffered from a rare virus in her spine and through physical therapy she's made an almost full recovery. Jessi surrendered to her "even if" and God chose to heal her. Some of us will not receive the healing we're hoping for from our "even if" situations. We can only make the best out of what God has given us, and in the meantime it's best to come up with a plan to adapt.

With Tom, I had to learn during his angry phase that words are very powerful, and I'd have to start choosing mine carefully to avoid triggering a meltdown. Caregivers should prepare a few stock responses to help comfort and assist our loved ones when they're struggling to communicate. Communication barriers are always frustrating, we would lose our patience too if we didn't know how to say what we wanted, needed, or felt. If we had to trust those around us to understand us. The key to avoiding this kind of frustration or de-escalating a situation if the frustration has already taken over, are *key phrases.*

I'm reminded of a time Tom asked a question and he got so mad at me that he shoved me away with an impressive force, if I do say so myself. I was absolutely stunned, and my first reaction was to cry or yell or walk away. It took me about 10 minutes to get my own emotions under control before I spoke. I wondered what I could have even said to cause this reaction. It occurred to me that Tom's emotional impulse control was deteriorating along with his memory. I would need to help guide him with that, as I would any of my children or grandchildren who were struggling with some big feelings of not feeling heard.

Choose phrases which you feel comfortable saying. Give them a chance and observe whether each phrase works or not. Tweak if necessary. Did you get the response for which you were hoping? Do you need to rephrase? Is that phrase altogether unhelpful and/or in need of retiring?

You can also derive your own key phrases from words or phrases to which your loved one gravitates. Observing what they are saying, how they are saying it, and why they may be saying what they're saying, will give you insight into their current state of emotional maturity. You will learn what's really important to them at that point.

The key phrases I'm providing you with are meant to give you a working model of things you can say when you feel a bit tongue tied. It may be helpful to memorize a few that look particularly useful, so you have something to try the next time things seem a bit tense. Add your own favorite phrases to the list as you come up with them.

- Thank you
- That's a thought
- That's one option; what's another one?
- Can you give me an example?
- Help me understand
- Let me say that another way
- What would success look like?
- Thank you for your feedback/Thank you for sharing your thoughts
- I understand
- Interesting…
- I couldn't help but notice
- If I ______would you______ (example: If I make a pie would you eat it?)
- (Practice) Yes, and…Instead of saying "no because," to everything, try saying "Yes, and." Here's an example: "No because I said so" or "Yes, and if we do that, it could break"
- It's okay to not be okay. It happens to everyone
- Is the TV too loud or can you hear it okay?
- What are you feeling? Seeing? Thinking? Worried about? Scared of?
- Are you worried about money? If they respond yes, explain finances to them "You taught me how to take care of our money and we are doing fine, the bills are all paid
- Replace "I just told you that. Don't you remember?" with" I'm sorry I thought I told you."
- Say me, my, or I instead of 'you'. Example: "You make it so difficult to…" instead try "I'm confused about the next step."
- How can I help you?

- Can you give me five minutes to finish this and then I will help you
- Would you like for me to…
- **Change "What hurts?" to "Where do you hurt?"**
- Feel, Felt, Found, "I know how you feel, **I have felt the same way.** What I found is…" Another way would be "I know how you feel **others have felt the same way** and…"
- I'm sorry
- I'm sorry I didn't hear; can you please say that again?
- How do you feel? How does that make you feel?
- Do you want A or B Do you want to wear the green or red shirt
- I love you
- You are my "guy"/" girl"
- You are NOT stupid
- The doctor will let us know when you can drive again
- That is 'our' car (not 'my' car)
- Are you hungry? Do you want this or that?
- Use please and thank you generously
- Can you please…
- (Tom)" I'm so stupid" (me) "No, you are forgetting some things but not from stupidity. I forget things too"

Chapter 15

Emotions Common to Dementia

I still remember a blustery fall day when my granddaughters were in their early teens. A fight between the two girls caused all-out physical warfare in my daughter's home. That resulted in slammed doors, tears, and screaming. I received a phone call from my eldest granddaughter that she simply couldn't be around her younger cousin any longer. I immediately got in my car and headed that way to try to make sense of teenage nonsense.

It is important to note that my granddaughters couldn't possibly be more different. Tori, my eldest, is an extrovert to the extreme, a go-getter, a direct-to-the-point person who doesn't bother sugar coating her opinion. She deeply feels her emotions, but—like myself and even my son (her father)—she keeps them pretty close to the vest. Jessi, my second granddaughter, is as much an introvert as Tori is an extravert. She's a sensitive, bookish homebody who can easily have her feathers ruffled by Tori's well-meaning directness. She—like her mother—is very prone to letting her emotions sit in the passenger seat.

I remember arriving to my daughter's empty house. The girls were old enough to be home alone and had planned a nice movie day with one another. A fight ensued. Its origin was as much a mystery to me as it was to them. One thing was for certain; both girls were irate with one another.

After recounting the shouting with each other which caused an actual physical fight, I watched their tear-stained faces as they looked expectantly to me for the solution. These are two of my most favorite girls in the world! I took a deep breath, summoning all the patience a person can manage when coming face-to-face with teenage ridiculousness, and willed myself not to laugh.

The fight itself was not funny, let me be clear. What *was* humorous to me, was my girls were simply showing on a smaller scale what many families ignore, until they're dealing with a major crisis like dementia. Then they must come together. The results can be conflict. Whether it is an old feud between siblings, resentment from children to their caregiving parent, or even a separated husband and wife needing to decide what's best for an in-law, conflict can complicate an already extremely difficult situation.

It is important to remember that when dealing with the business of dementia and the family matters associated, conflict cannot be an elephant in the room. As Susan Forward, Ph.D. has said; "Denial is the most primitive and the most powerful of psychological defenses." I personally have taken it another step further from experience: Denial is your *enemy*. Ignoring the problems among your family early on in your dementia journey will only let them stew and explode when everyone is in the most need of being on one page. During your loved one's final days, or in your grief process, it is not the time to try and fix these wounds. It is imperative to seek counseling, have a very direct discussion of conflicts among each other with a trusted mediator, or just plain old forgiveness and *letting it go* is the best strategy. Attempt to mobilize the family into crisis mode together, so that you can all handle things as they come, efficiently and cooperatively.

When conflict resolution is not possible at that time, I refer to a formula to help relieve some of the pressure: E+R=O.

Event + Reaction= Outcome. Just as you saw in the example I've provided of the conflict between my granddaughters, your reaction to the conflict or event can be more important than the event itself in ensuring a positive outcome. When I was attempting to diffuse the situation with my granddaughters, I made absolutely sure that I maintained a calm demeanor and a listening ear. Once both sides assured me they were finished speaking, I reminded them that they were putting a black eye on the face of our Savior by attempting to hurt one another. I explained we were to love others as we love ourselves, especially when those others are our family. The outcome was both girls taking some time to cool down and making up later that day. If I had met them at their level, who knows what would have happened.

This formula is the absolute bread and butter of the caregiver when dealing with the emotions of, not only their loved ones as they begin to lose control over their feelings through the progression of their disease, but also to keep the peace during those times of tension between family members. Remember the importance of conflict resolution and diffusion with those around your loved one. Arguing or tense environments can worsen the dementia patient's ability to remain at an emotional equilibrium and cause unnecessary anxiety or even depression.

This should go without saying, but if there is a conflict, the people involved need to de-escalate immediately, or leave. If a disagreement cannot be dealt with in a low key and peaceable manner, they should not be spoken about at all. This risks adding stress to your loved one who is already in a state of constant anxiety due to their dementia.

When it comes to the emotional health of your loved one on their dementia journey, a wide range of emotions are normal to experience, for both the loved one and the caregiver. The emotions can change day-to-day and in the later stages it can be minute-to-minute.

Happiness can precede weeping, and weeping can turn into uncontrollable laughter. It is common to feel like you're drowning in intense waves of emotions—whether it be your loved one's or your own.

Our loved one cannot control their emotions, so it is critical that we, as the caregivers, control ours and not join in on a downward emotional spiral. There are often clues and non-verbal's that we can pay attention to which will let us know what's coming. If we suspect there is a change coming, we can be proactive and intentional in our response.

Emotions common to dementia

- Anger
- Quiet
- Silent
- Scared
- Denial
- Can't do anything
- Grieving
- Acceptance
- Excessive crying
- Unexplained laughter
- Happiness
- Sadness
- Quiet resignation
- Out of control
- Panic

Ways emotions can manifest themselves in the behavior of your loved one

- Moving objects around
- Forget family members and names
- See things which are not there
- Not eating
- Overeating or forgetting they've just had a meal
- Pacing

- Changing clothes multiple times in a day
- Following caregiver everywhere
- Sleeping longer than normal
- Talking to themselves
- Hiding
- Wondering off
- Loss of reality
- Thinking TV characters were real
- Inappropriately affectionate
- Profanity
- Unable to take care of basic hygiene
- Rambling
- Aggressiveness
- Weird noises

Chapter 16

Tough Discussions – The Talk

Tom and I were married right as we both crossed the threshold from children to adults. You could say we grew up together. We were like childhood best friends who continued to grow and love each other for the rest of Tom's life, and I know he will be my one and only romantic love on this earth. Our soles are tied together in a love that is both the stuff of soulmates, and of the strongest, most deeply rooted friendship.

Of my many favorite things to do with Tom, was to put our heads together and make decisions. My favorite decision we ever made together was to say I do. That choice is closely followed by when we chose to become parents; to put down roots; to buy a home; to prioritize our finances by saving and investing wisely; to be good stewards of what God had given us as He commanded. We decided early in our marriage to serve the Lord, and I don't regret one second of time, one penny spent, one drop of sweat given in sacrifice to fulfill our mutual promise to our Heavenly Father. Tom and I had a deep love for supporting missionaries, a love that lasted in Tom for almost the entirety of his disease. One of his final wishes was actually for mourners to donate to missionaries in lieu of flowers. I remember times that he would become anxious and couldn't quite put a finger on why. Through open-ended questions, it was always determined that he was afraid our generous payments to the missionaries would be forgotten and they wouldn't get their money. Oh, my goodness, did I just adore his big heart!

Some decisions through the process of our lives together were no-brainers, like the ones I listed above. Some of them were much harder. When my job began to provide the opportunity to travel abroad, Tom and I tossed around the decisions about whether he would accompany me. A trip to Russia and later Poland was in the works, and Tom was *not* pleased to know that I planned on following through with them. We knew there was significant unrest between countries at the time. He knew from years of experience that once I'd set my mind to something, it was wiser to just leave me to my adventurous notions than try to fight them. The thing Tom fixated upon was his complete unwillingness to accompany me.

After many months of impasse between us, Tom's protective spirit outweighed his desire to win the battle of wills, and we decided that we *would* be traveling together. To Tom's delight and also dismay, we had an amazing time together! It was an absolute dream come true to adventure alongside my favorite person.

Tom and I traveled to many countries together, each time more fun than the last and I will forever be glad we made the decision not to live out of fear.

One of the hardest decisions I ever had to make pre-dementia, was when Tom was in his motorcycle accident. For almost six weeks, the doctors insisted that Tom's leg would need to be amputated. Tom refused to take this lying down…. Figuratively speaking of course, since he spent almost 24/7 laying down at that time.

I remember as the doctors began a surgery in an attempt to save Tom's leg, as he so desperately wanted. I was asked to stand directly outside the operating room in case an emergency consent form needed to be signed to give permission to amputate his leg if that was the only way to save his life. This was my first choice in years that I was forced to make without my other half. I desperately wished I could talk to Tom, to ask him what he wanted. I remember how anxious I was through the whole surgery, not only for my husband's safety, but what if I made a decision that didn't honor what he wanted?

Thankfully, Tom's leg was saved and he later learned how to walk. He had to have many surgeries on his leg over the years, each serving as a reminder of that terrifying day when I awaited a worst-case-scenario and a decision that I didn't know how to make..

I thought of this day when I had to make the decision to take Tom's driving privileges away. He'd gotten in an accident just up the street from our house and thankfully, no one was hurt. Once that happened, I realized that not only could we be sued or jailed for letting a known dementia patient continue to drive, Tom could also hurt or kill himself or others. The decision had to be made—my first decision without my love in decades—to do what was best for the people around us, and Tom by extension.

If I thought the anxiety of Tom's surgery many years before was bad, the anxiety associated with this decision was easily a million times harder. I was in essence taking Tom's last little bit of freedom away, and I knew that, just like with the prospect of losing his legs, Tom would not be giving this up without a fight. From a strike of genius, I decided to hand his doctor a note at Tom's next check up asking him to tell Tom he could no longer drive.

As expected, Tom was absolutely furious. I remember many times he would shout or just dejectedly mumble "I'm not living like this.". We both knew Tom had no decision but to live like this, but it didn't stop Tom from sinking into quite a depression and even sometimes rage.

There was a day that Tom decided to hide my spare keys to sneak out and drive when I wasn't paying attention. The problem was that once I noticed they were gone, he'd already forgotten where he'd hidden them. By the grace of God, his dementia had somehow prevented him from putting himself and others on the road in an extreme amount of danger. I knew I could no longer leave keys where Tom could find them, and my spares would have to be left with my daughter for both safe keeping and emergencies.

The worst thing we faced in our four-year journey, were the discussions and decisions that had to take place. When we got the official diagnosis, my heart felt like it had exploded and left the scene, all at the same time. First, I wished it could go away. I wished I could pretend it wasn't there, and keep my best friend for just a little while longer. My instinct was to not talk about it or tell anyone until we had to, in order to keep my little bubble of denial for as long as possible. I know today, for our family, that would have been a mistake.

Hard decisions and conversations took place at a pace that worked for us. Nothing was left unsaid. Nothing was hidden in the closet. In the early stages, I got to make decisions with my very best friend for the final few times. Instead of life affirming, happy choices, we were now planning for Tom's imminent decline and even death. Was it painful? Yes. Do I have any regrets? No. I was 100% honest with Tom, and he with me. Was it scary? Yes, at times. By being open and candid with him, he was free to ask questions, share his fears, cry and return our love to his fullest capacity. As I reflect back to those discussions I can smile and say, "I wouldn't have changed anything."

Early decisions that must be made

- Going for the official evaluation
- The actual diagnosis
- The Future
- Driving/State ID
- Keep them at home or nursing home
- Money/finances
- Family meeting, team approach
- Medical team
- (DNR) Do Not Resuscitate decision
- Final Arrangements (Funeral Planning)

Chapter 17

Decisions to Be Made

From the day our sweet Tami was born, Tom was instantly smitten. She was his girl, and he was her guy. It was like they had their own language, understanding one another in a way no one else could: Tom simply adored Tami.

It was out of love that Tom decided Tami would be dependent on absolutely no one, not even for car repairs. Whenever it was even slightly warm enough, you could find Tom outside giving Tami yet another lesson on car maintenance. To this day, Tami's favorite thing about Tom is how easy he was to talk to, and how he took care of her.

Tom even tried to take care of Tami when it wasn't necessarily in her best interest. When Tami first married my wonderful, kind-hearted, devoted son-in-law Tony, he was not unlike her father. He worked a lot and spent a lot of his spare time playing sports. Tami was perplexed. She had expected a close friendship full of conversation, affection, and love with her new husband. As newlyweds often do, Tami and Tony began having quite a bit of trouble seeing eye to eye. Our strong, opinionated, sensitive girl, who absolutely recoiled at the slightest bit of conflict, had little to no tolerance for rejection. Eventually she found herself in our living room uncontrollably weeping and begging that we let her come home.

"Let's go get your stuff," Tom declared. "I'll let you come home, dolly."

I cleared my throat and saw two equally hot-tempered faces glaring back at me. "Tami, you can't come home." I stated as matter-of-factly as I could manage.

"Mom-"Tami started

"Anita, of course she can come home!" Tom cried, aghast that I would deny my own daughter respite with us.

"Tami, this is fixable," I said evenly. "You have to go home and work your way through this. You can't fix your marriage from your parents' house."

"But Mom," Tami whimpered, looking so much like my sweet, innocent little girl that it was hard not to lose my nerve. "I feel like he just doesn't know how to love me at all."

"Then you need to teach him how to love you." I said simply.

I am happy to say that this coming year, Tami and Tony will celebrate 32 years of marriage. They put in the work as Tom and I had, and their marriage has blossomed beyond belief. I knew Tami, of all people, with her loving and empathetic heart, would be perfectly capable of helping her husband grow into the partner she so desperately wanted. Tony with his unwavering loyalty and tender-hearted spirit, would forever protect and cherish my daughter.

The point of this story is to tell you that what we, as caregivers, want to do on instinct, is not necessarily what is best. Tom wanted to protect Tami and bring her home into his loving arms to save her from the heartache she was experiencing. But what was best, was to support her in returning to her home and working on her marriage. Knowing that we were right behind her and ready to catch her if she fell, enabled her to return to her home.

Tami, knowing how her daddy always shielded her from harm to the best of his ability, struggled especially as he began to become more and more lost from her as his disease progressed. One story I believe will haunt my daughter until her dying days, was when she was sitting outside enjoying a gentle spring breeze with Tom and he began to grab his head and plead "Please, help me! Something is wrong, I need you to help me!"

Tami's striking green eyes filled with tears, "I can't dad, I can't help you," she sniffed.

"I would do anything to help you! Please, help me!" Tom lamented, not understanding that there was nothing any of us could do, except walk him home.

Some decisions can only be made by a caregiver and their family. Some choices can be made by the family with the loved one's input. It is important to know that as dementia reaches its late and final stages, virtually all choices will fall to you as a caregiver and your surrounding loved ones. It is at this point that I will remind you that we all—like Tom—will want to do the most protective, life preserving thing possible, but our instinct may not always be what's best.

One question I kept in the back of my mind was, "If I do ______ will it improve the quality of Tom's life?" The ________ can be filled in with many things. An example is "If I have Tom take another four-hour Dementia assessment, will it improve the quality of his life?" If no, then don't put him through it.

Another decision that was incredibly difficult to make was the decision to stop feeding Tom and giving him anything to drink as he approached his final days of life. I believe God put the right professionals in charge of Tom's care, and they instructed us that if we fed Tom in his unresponsive state, he would likely choke to death because his body had already begun to shut down and he could no longer chew or swallow.

Tami, Ty and I, with my granddaughter, Jessi sat around Tom as we watched him slowly leave us, all of us knowing we were thinking the same thing: how can we just let him die? How could we not advocate for him more? Why didn't we try to feed him? Maybe he'd surprise us all and be able to eat? Our instinct was to nurture and care for Tom's body, but his soul had made the decision to vacate it long before this time, and any attempts to save Tom would ultimately be futile and do more harm than good.

Our oldest grandchild, Tori, arrived unexpectedly a few minutes before Tom took his last breath. She rushed to his side and whispered "Popah it's Tori, I'm Here". And with that, Tom departed to Heaven. It was as if he waited for her. Tori cried and said, "I wanted him to walk me down the isle when I get married". Tami quickly said, "Popah was with you when you drew your first breath, and you were with him as he drew his last breath." God wastes nothing, not even where everyone is at an appointed time.

Jessi has shared before that her instinct as she watched her beloved Popah take his dying breaths was to shout, "don't leave me!" at the top of her lungs, to throw herself on him, to do something to bring him back to her. But she knew that what was best for Tom—and his soul—was to let it depart in peace.

It is important to categorize decisions by which should be made with your loved one, which should be made with your family, and which should be made for you personally. Tom was very close with our children and of course our grandchildren, but Tom's heart was tied to my own. God blessed me with this man, and I was given the heavy responsibility and deepest honor to make every decision regarding the walk of my love to his eternal home with his best interest in mind.

Caregivers, please remember that dementia is "the long walk home." We all know how it ends. There will be some decisions you make to improve quality of life, some decisions to protect your household and finances, and even decisions about how your loved one is to die. Remember that you are the final say in what happens with your loved one and their final days here on earth. As the bible says; "pray about everything." When you are making these lonely decisions, remember that God is with you for every step, and consult him when you are unsure.

Common personal decisions for caregivers

- When do I (the caregiver) retire? Can we afford for me to retire?
- When do we need an attorney?
- What should I do, when I can no longer leave him/her alone?
- Do I have someone to be a co-caregiver with me? (Family member, friend, volunteer)
- How long can he/she drive? How do I handle him/her not driving?
- When do I get him/her a state ID vs. driving license?
- When do I take over the expenses/finances? How much money do I give him/her to keep on their person or spend as they like?
- When do I discuss a (DNR) Do Not Resuscitate with my loved one?   With the family? With the kids? When do I sign it?
- When do I contact Pallia care?
- When do I contact Hospice?

Chapter 18

The Fog

I remember the last several weeks of Tom's life, there was a hospital bed in the middle of our living room so Tom would be close by and not isolated during the day. I began to feel like I was no longer in my house. I felt a desperation to "get my house back" but I didn't know how to put my finger on what was exactly making my house no longer feel like a home.

I realized that the reason I no longer felt at home here was because, from the very beginning of my life with Tom, our homes were filled with laughter and love and silliness. Now our home was mostly filled with a thick silence that one could slice through with a steak knife.

As Tom passed, I didn't find myself distraught with grief but rather incumbered by a fog. A fog that took over, a fog that surrounded, a fog that invaded my very mind.

I felt overtaken by this sort of weighty mist that kept me frozen, longing for a "home" that felt lost to me, even as I sat inside it. I missed the jovial atmosphere that usually filled the halls of any dwelling my family inhabited. How could I get that back? Was that even possible?

I looked around at all the broken, empty faces around me. Faces of people I'd snuggled as babies, comforted as small children, played cards with as teens, some of which I now guided as adults. They were all missing someone who'd been a fixture in their lives. Tom was in every one of our children, grandchildren, and great grandchildren's lives for their *entire* lives.

Even the significant others of my children and grandchildren were utterly distraught. I watched as my granddaughter, Jessi's husband tried aimlessly to soothe his sobbing wife. My grandson Zane's fiancé, Kylie, attempted with great courage, to pull words from his pursed lips as his jaws quivered, a motion I knew from experience meant he was trying to hold back tears. My son-in-law, Tony looked as dejected as a person could, mourning the man he'd seen as a second father, disbelief coloring his face as he tried to process that Tom was truly gone.

Everywhere I looked, I saw despair, and that was only natural. Only I knew that this would devastate Tom. He wouldn't have been able to bear watching every one of our heartbeats in the throws of despair at his death. He would want them to rejoice that he was finally receiving the ultimate healing and reuniting with his parents, with my parents, with his very close friend and my sister's husband, Dave.

Being the matriarch of a family grieving its patriarch, is a helpless ache in and of itself, but to add insult to injury I felt suspended mid-air, floating above an abyss of never-ending grief and being held there by this thick, all consuming, strangling fog.

I realized then that my only lifeline to clearing the fog, to getting my feeling of home back, to keep my wits about me as I led my family through their loss while not even knowing what lie ahead myself— was to go back to the purpose I've always felt God placed over my life. I was meant to love, serve, and help others.

By the time Tom passed, I'd already been writing my blog, "dementia diaries", for almost 2 years. It started off as an internal challenge to me, and it later became a way to cope with Tom's ever declining condition. I had felt a "God nudge" to keep it going since the very first time I posted anything related to my journey as a caregiver and as a wife to a person with dementia. I'd originally thought I'd be posting a one-time update, and "dementia diaries" became so much more.

"Dementia Diaries" became a means of connecting myself with others who were behind me on their journey with dementia themselves, to speak life into them, to encourage them, to give them direction on their path.... to *help* them.

I began holding caregiver calls, a thing I still do to this day. I invite everyone to join in on zoom weekly. Sometimes 10-15 people hop on, and a discussion table ensues. I'm brought back to simpler times of conducting corporate meetings and listening to colleagues share their opinions. Sometimes no one joins the call, and I know the Lord has set aside some time for us to be in fellowship with one another, because He has some things to say to me. More often than not, 1 person will hop on the call at the exact time that they feel completely bogged down by the responsibility of caregiving and the privilege of walking someone home, although that doesn't exactly feel like a privilege. These are the times I must confess I like most, because it is an opportunity for me to minister to someone in desperate need to be seen, to be heard, to be *understood.*

In "the fog" is where my idea to write this book began. I knew I needed to refer back to what God put me on this earth to do, to *help.* I had already been asked by numerous other caregivers to take the many lists I comprised on "Dementia Diaries" and put them all in one place to reference. I realized caregivers just now reading my blogs would also not have easy access to lists/insights I had already shared in the past. I realized that "if not me, who?" and decided to gift caregivers with something I wished I'd had: a survival guide. That survival guide is in your hands. I must say, every moment I spent tirelessly working, every late night I spent gathering notes, every ream of paper I used to print every "Dementia Diaries" I'd ever penned, they were all worth it because you—my dearest caregiver—are receiving the help and direction I so desperately desired when I walked this path before you.

In the next few chapters are challenges I feel are of the utmost importance for caregivers and will help you to reframe and refocus when needed during the many trying times ahead. I encourage and beseech you to please take these challenges and wholeheartedly throw yourself into them. You have no idea how much you will cling to your very own words when times are tough.

Chapter 19

Caregivers' Challenges

Challenge #1

A few days ago, I received a phone call from a frantic caregiver. She started by saving, "I hate my husband." I took a moment to collect my thoughts before muscle memory from over 30 years of corporate coaching took over, and I began asking her several questions as if I were speaking to an upper manager in need of guidance to properly run their team:

1) Did you love your husband when you married him?
2) Did he love you?
3) How long have you been married?
4) Have you had a good marriage? "So, it sounds like you loved your husband, and you shared a great marriage and life together, right?"
5) If that's true, do you now hate him or Dementia?

Long pause, "Wow, I never thought of it that way." We continued talking and I asked her to accept a challenge. It is the same challenge I am asking you to take now.

A) Make a list (I strongly recommend using a journal) of why you married your spouse. Answer the five questions listed above. Work on your list for a few days to make sure you have a clear picture of the situation. Think about your thoughts, feelings, and actions to this point in time.

If you are a caregiver for other than a spouse, answer these questions:

1) How long have I known this person?

2)   What is our relationship?

3)   Why am I doing this?

4)   Did I start out happy to be able to be his/her caregiver?

5)   Am I sorry I took this on?

6)   Work on your list for several days. Think about your thoughts, feelings, emotions, and actions to this point in time.

The last step is to determine what you need to do in the future to keep yourself motivated to continue in this role. Answer the following:

1)   What action(s) do I need to take?

2)   Who do I need to encourage to help me?

3)   What comments could you change to make them positive in the future (i.e., "you just asked me that" Could change to "Is there something on your mind that I can help you with?"

Caregiver Challenge #2

Some of the emotions and worries experienced by caregivers include: health, loneliness, regret, no one to talk to, frequent changes, sadness, loss of friends, their safety and that of their loved one, loved one getting lost, isolation, resentment, loss of independence, hatred of loved one (both ways), abuse (both ways) guilt, and other things that are indescribable. These things are real and typically kept inside consciously or unconsciously.

The list above is not about things or feeling these things, it is about what we do with these thoughts. The challenge I would like for you to consider is:

Make a list of your strengths and 'developmental needs'. Notice I did not say strengths and weaknesses. Often what we consider a weakness is just something that you need to develop, perhaps not having to use that skill in the past.

So, you need two lists: 1) list your strengths and 2) list of your developmental needs. Do your best not to just write the opposites across from each other (use two sheets). Take several days to complete the list and add to it whenever a new thought comes to mind.

Once you have carefully made two lists, think about them, and come up with an action plan for dealing with them as you feel them. One response would be to use a strength or try something totally different. Who might you need to talk to (a coach, friend, mentor, pastor, health advisor, social worker, etc.) give you advice or help?

Caregiver Challenge #3

The first time I felt "down" and wondered what would help me, I started a list of things I am thankful for. My list has grown to over 80 things and has been indispensable when I was in desperate need of reframing and a nice injection of positivity.

☐ I challenge you to start a **List of Thankfulness or Gratitude**, things for which you are thankful.
☐ Work on your list for 21 days until it becomes a habit.
☐ Revisit the list at least 'weekly' and add to the list.

Chapter 20

Caregiver Affirmations

Our thoughts can encourage us or defeat us. As our loved one declines it can be too easy to let our guard down and before we know it, we are attending our own pity party.

To avoid the trap of negativity and self-pity, there are things we can say to ourselves to help us avoid "pity party" thinking. This list of affirmations is not an exhaustive list, so feel free to add to it regularly.

Copy the affirmations or transfer your favorite ones to 3x5 index cards. Put them where you see them every day (refrigerator, bathroom mirror, at your desk, etc.) Don't just notice them each day, read some out loud and smile at yourself.

- I was created for a purpose
- I trust God, the 'great physician'
- I am ready to take on any and all challenges that I face today
- I am living my legacy
- God has entrusted my loved one to my care and I will do the best I can, for as long as I can
- I am enough for this responsibility
- I am bold enough to ask God for more blessings that I could ever imagine
- I am of unimaginable worth and value
- I am confident in who I am and trust myself to live my true potential
- I will live with intention
- I will advocate for my loved one both for health and finances

- I will be the voice for my loved one
- I will forgive and be forgiven when I am wrong
- I am more than my past mistakes
- I am empowered to release my shame and guilt
- God is always on my side and walks with me daily
- I will never lose hope
- I trust God to go through this with me
- I will make decisions that I can live with, with no regrets
- I will ask for help when needed and not let my pride to take over
- I will surround myself with positive people
- I will appreciate those who support me
- I will listen more than I talk
- I will listen with my ears, eyes, and heart
- I will thank God each day for being with me

Important Things to Do (condensed list)

1. Make sure all bank and credit union accounts have direct or joint beneficiaries. (All bank accounts should be joint at this point. If they are not already, your mortgage and car titles can be joint as well). The beneficiaries need only go to the bank with death certificate and an ID of their own.

2. Transfer on Death (TOD) deed if you own a home. Completing this document allows you to transfer ownership of your home to your designee. All they have to do is take their ID and the death certificate to the county building and the deed is signed over. Doing this will avoid the home having to go through probate.

3. Living Will: Allows you to put In writing exactly what you want done in the event you cannot speak for yourself when it comes to health decisions.

4. Durable Power of Attorney: Allows one to designate a person to make financial or legal decisions. If one is no longer competent to do so.

5. Power of Attorney (POA): Allows one to designate a person to make healthcare decisions the person.

6. Last Will and Testament designates to whom personal belongings will go to at the time of your death.

7. Funeral Planning Declaration: allows one to say exactly what one wishes as far as disposition of the body and services.

8. If the above documents are completed, hopefully you can avoid probate. If all of the above is not done, you have to open an estate account at the bank. All money that doesn't have direct beneficiaries goes into this account. You have to have an attorney to open the estate account. The attorney also has to publicize your passing in the newspaper or post publication at the county courthouse, to allow anyone to make a claim on your property.

9. Make a list of all banks and account numbers, all investment institutions with account numbers, lists of credit cards, utility accounts, etc. Leave clear instructions as to how and when these things are paid. Make sure heirs knows where life insurance policies are located.

10. Make 100% sure someone knows your apple ID, bank ID account logins and passwords

11. Make sure you have titles for all vehicles, campers, motorcycles, etc.

12. Most Importantly, talk with those closest to you and make all your wishes known. Talk to those whom you designated, as well as those close to you whom you did not designate. Do this to explain why your decisions were made and to avoid lingering questions or hurt feelings

Chapter 21

Epilogue - The Fog Lifts

I sit in my three-season room, across a table from my granddaughter, Jessi. We are discussing grief, struggles, joys, and pitfalls of our journey with our dearly-missed Tom. We discuss our different grief processes and how happy we are to have had the tribe God chose to help us through.

Looking back on the fog that I felt trapped inside for weeks after Tom was gone. Now I realize it was for a purpose. It is difficult to tell a grieving or overwhelmed caregiver "I know how you feel" unless you've been there yourself.

Mine and Jessi's grief periods were much different from one another. She was devastated and retreated within herself to nurse her wounds. When she was ready, she went to therapy to try and connect with some happy memories of her Popah, and to process this void in her life. I asked her when she felt her grief lift—not entirely, but to a bearable amount.

"I started reading a book series Popah and I both loved. I used my special bookmark with his picture and obituary on it, and I realized I had so many fun memories of watching the movies and borrowing the books from him. I didn't feel overwhelmed with how much I missed him; I was able to simply smile at his memory."

As I began wrapping up the final touches of this book, I am reminded of a similar story. When I was still in the depths of my "fog", I began to feel a peace that surmounted all understanding. I felt warmth and comfort in the knowledge that my Tom was well again, he knew who his family was, and he was keeping my seat warm in heaven much like when he saved our second-row seats for us in church each morning. I could feel almost a light sensation of embrace, and it seemed to lift my fog with every passing day.

I know now that I was feeling the comfort of my Heavenly Father. I was resting in His embrace, and He was lifting my fog as I surrendered it to Him. He was easing my burden, and the relief was so sweet. I began to think only of the Tom from our younger years, of the silly, bold, hard-working best friend of mine who walked through every experience of this life by my side.

I know through the hope of my Savior and my belief in Him that I will be reunited with Tom one day. I may ache for him sometimes, but I know that one day the Lord will call me back home to be with Him, and with my Tom.

"Even so, it is well with my soul."

APPENDIX

These check-lists are meant to be a handy reference so you can keep track of what has or has not been done.

Have a fireproof/waterproof folder or box for

    ☐ Medical cards

    ☐ Vaccine cards

    ☐ List of Medications with dosage, how many times a day, and what time of day they should be taken

    ☐ Social Security Card

    ☐ Driver's License or State ID

    ☐ Legal paperwork, Power of Attorney and an up-to-date will

    ☐ Make sure the will is up-to-date with one or more of the children, and/or a substitute, listed on it to make medical and financial decisions

Caregiver Bag for a Hospital or Emergency room visit (to grab quickly)

    ☐ Phone and charger

    ☐ iPad/tablet/computer, iWatch and charger

    ☐ Your medication (if any) and loved one's medicine (or list mentioned above)

    ☐ Extension cord, paper & pens, reading glasses

    ☐ Bible and other reading material

Items for Home Use

    ☐ Baby monitor/camera, baby wipes, chux pads - (Disposable and washable)

    ☐ Disposable gloves

    ☐ Large, glow in the dark house number on home or mailbox (for emergency vehicles to see easily)

    ☐ Antibacterial soap and disinfectant wipes

☐ Rinse free hair and bath sponges or wipes (by Scrubzz)

☐ Phone numbers for doctors secured to the refrigerator

☐ List of bills that need to be paid

☐ Passwords for credit cards, e-bill pay, phone, computer, etc.

☐ Pill Holder

☐ Silicone placemat for table (by Upward Baby)

☐ First Aid Kit

☐ Pill container and pill splitter

☐ Waterproof mattress pad

☐ Disposable leak proof pads

Medical Bag for home use

☐ Blood pressure cuff and batteries

☐ Thermometer

☐ Kardia heart monitor (use with phone) (Amazon)

☐ Pulse Oximeter to measure oxygen levels (finger)

Trunk/car Emergency Bag

☐ Diapers/Pull Ups/clean underwear

☐ Baby wipes, disinfectant wipes, rinse free wash clothes, paper towels, chux pads, disposal gloves, plastic bags (for wet clothes)

☐ Change of clothes: shirt, pants, socks, undershirt, shoes, towel, bottle of water (don't ask me why I know this)

The business of death, have copies of:

☐ Social Security Card

☐ Birth certificate

☐ Marriage License (if applicable)

☐ Military ID and DD214

☐ State ID or Driver's License

Helpful hints

    ☐ Notify pharmacist of who has permission to pick up prescriptions (more than one person is helpful)

    ☐ Notify family doctor who to contact; loved one must sign authorization form, do this early in the diagnosis

Important Things to Do

    ☐ Make sure all bank and credit union accounts have direct or joint beneficiaries. (All bank accounts should be joint at this point. If they are not already, your mortgage and car titles can be joint as well). The beneficiaries need only go to the bank with death certificate and an ID of their own.

    ☐ Transfer on Death (TOD) deed if you own a home. Completing this document allows you to transfer ownership of your home to your designee. All they have to do is take their ID and the death certificate to the county building and the deed is signed over. Doing this will avoid the home having to go through probate.

    ☐ Living Will: Allows you to put In writing exactly what you want done in the event you cannot speak for yourself when it comes to health decisions.

    ☐ Durable Power of Attorney: Allows one to designate a person to make financial or legal decisions. If one is no longer competent to do so.

    ☐ Power of Attorney (POA): Allows one to designate a person to make healthcare decisions the person.

    ☐ Last Will and Testament designates to whom personal belongings will go to at the time of your death.

☐	Funeral Planning Declaration: allows one to say exactly what one wishes as far as disposition of the body and services.

☐	If the above documents are completed, hopefully you can avoid probate. If all of the above is not done, you have to open an estate account at the bank. All money that doesn't have direct beneficiaries goes into this account. You have to have an attorney to open the estate account. The attorney also has to publicize your passing in the newspaper or post publication at the county courthouse, to allow anyone to make a claim on your property.

☐	Make a list of all banks and account numbers, all investment institutions with account numbers, lists of credit cards, utility accounts, etc. Leave clear instructions as to how and when these things are paid. Make sure heirs knows where life insurance policies are located.

☐	Make 100% sure someone knows your apple ID, bank ID account logins and passwords.

☐	Make sure you have titles for all vehicles, campers, motorcycles, etc.

☐	Most Importantly, talk with those closest to you and make all your wishes known. Talk to those whom you designated, as well as those close to you whom you did not designate. Do this to explain why your decisions were made and to avoid lingering questions or hurt feelings.

Additional Resources

Anita Yelton is an accomplished speaker and business coach. She writes a daily post on Facebook called Dementia Diaries for all those who need a word of encouragement. In addition, she does a monthly live chat on Saturday mornings. For more information reach out through her Facebook at Anita Yelton and read her encouraging posts entitled Dementia Diaries.